SPOTLIGHT ON
IMMIGRATION AND MIGRATION

# ANTI-SEMITISM

JEWISH IMMIGRANTS SEEK SAFETY IN AMERICA (1881–1914)

Dava Pressberg

**PowerKiDS**
press.

NEW YORK

Published in 2016 by The Rosen Publishing Group, Inc.
29 East 21st Street, New York, NY 10010

Editor: Caitie McAneney
Book Design: Samantha DeMartin / Andrea Davison-Bartolotta

Photo Credits: Cover, p. 12 courtesy of the Library of Congress; p. 4 Hulton Archive/Getty Images; p. 5 Leemage/ Universal Images Group/Getty Images; p. 6 DEA/A. Dagli Orti/Getty Images; pp. 7, 19, 21 Jewish Chronicle/ Heritage Images/Getty Images; pp. 8, 16 Everett Historical/Shutterstock.com; pp. 8–9 North Wind Picture Archives; pp. 11, 14 Universal History Archive/UIG via Getty Images; p. 13 Apic/Getty Images; p. 15 Chris Parypa Photography/Shutterstock.com; pp. 17, 20 Buyenlarge/Getty Images; pp. 18–19 Lewis W. Hines/Buyenlarge/ Getty Images; p. 22 Bruce Yuanyue Bi/Getty Images.

Library of Congress Cataloging-in-Publication Data

Pressberg, Dava, author.
 Anti-Semitism : Jewish immigrants seek safety in America (1881-1914) / Dava Pressberg.
    pages cm — (Spotlight on immigration and migration)
 Includes index.
 ISBN 978-1-5081-4051-1 (pbk.)
 ISBN 978-1-5081-4052-8 (6 pack)
 ISBN 978-1-5081-4054-2 (library binding)
 1. Antisemitism—Russia (Federation) 2. Jews, Russian—United States. 3. Jews, Russian—Migrations. 4. Jewish refugees—United States. I. Title.
 DS146.R9P725 2016
 305.892'407309034—dc23
                                        2015023450

Manufactured in the United States of America

CPSIA Compliance Information: Batch #BW16PK: For further information contact Rosen Publishing, New York, New York at 1-800-237-9932.

# CONTENTS

# FREEDOM IN THE UNITED STATES

For **persecuted** people around the world, the United States has long held the promise of freedom and a better future. Since the late 1700s, many American citizens have been free to follow their religious and political beliefs. They've also been free to migrate, or move from place to place, and to settle and work where they please. People in countries all over the world heard of this freedom and were drawn to the United States.

Some **immigrants** came from places where they had no say in how their government ran their country. Others came from places where they were persecuted for their religious beliefs. From 1881 to 1914, more than 2 million Jews came to the United States from Russia. In the United States, they hoped to find freedom of religion and a fair political system.

The Jewish migration from Russia to America was just one of several waves of Jewish immigration. In the 1840s, many German Jews left their homeland because of a poor economy and persecution. Even more Jews came from Germany before World War I broke out.

# ANTI-SEMITISM IN RUSSIA

For thousands of years, Jews have lived in settlements of their own people in countries all over the world. During the 1700s, there were large Jewish communities in Russia. This was a time when Russia was becoming a powerful empire by conquering neighboring lands.

It was also a time when **anti-Semitism** in Russia was widespread. By the early 1800s, the Russian government had created laws that limited Jewish people's rights. For example, Jews were only allowed to live in a certain area, known as the Pale of Settlement. Fueled by the anti-Semitism that existed, Russians sometimes led attacks against Jews called pogroms (POH-gruhmz). These **violent** attacks killed many Jews and forced others to flee the country for safety.

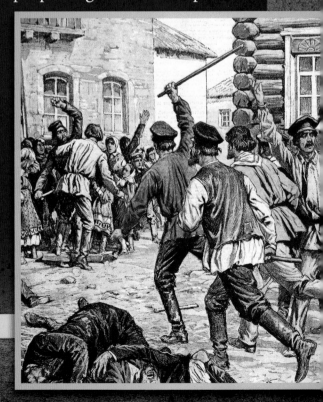

A POGROM IN RUSSIA

Between 1881 and 1884, Russians raided Jewish homes and businesses. Even bloodier pogroms occurred between 1903 and 1906. In this picture, Jewish men look at copies of their sacred religious books that were ruined during a pogrom.

# TEMPORARY LAWS

Alexander II was the czar, or emperor, of Russia in the mid-1800s. However, terrorists killed him on March 13, 1881. After his death, anti-Semitism became even more widespread. Many Russians blamed the Jews for his death. In the unrest that followed the czar's death, pogroms became more common. Hundreds of Jews were killed during this time.

**CZAR ALEXANDER II**

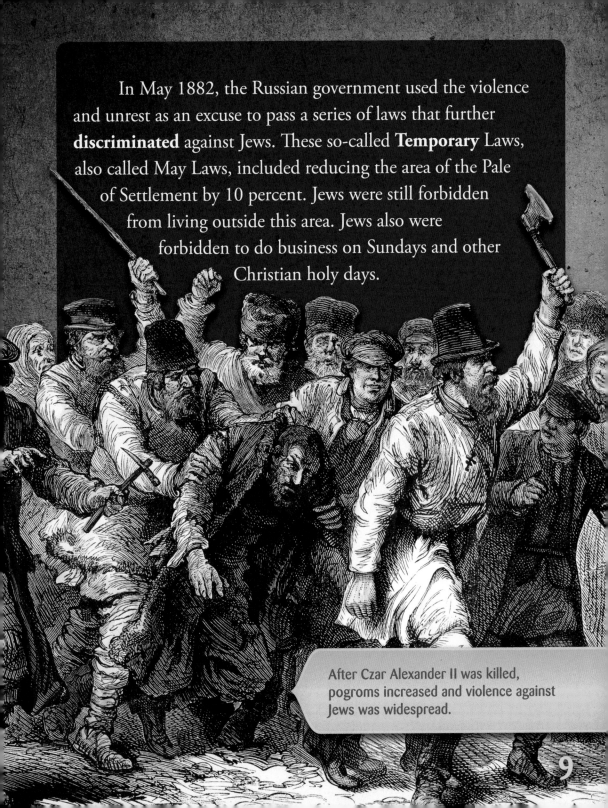

In May 1882, the Russian government used the violence and unrest as an excuse to pass a series of laws that further **discriminated** against Jews. These so-called **Temporary** Laws, also called May Laws, included reducing the area of the Pale of Settlement by 10 percent. Jews were still forbidden from living outside this area. Jews also were forbidden to do business on Sundays and other Christian holy days.

After Czar Alexander II was killed, pogroms increased and violence against Jews was widespread.

# FLEEING RUSSIA

Over time, it became clear that Russia was no longer a place of safety, freedom, or opportunity. Many Jews decided they had to leave Russia. They began to hear stories about the opportunities that existed in America.

However, leaving Russia was not easy in the late 1800s. The Russian government made it hard for people to get **passports** to leave the country. It was even harder for the Jews, whose movement was especially **restricted** by the government. Officially, Jews were restricted from travel. Unofficially, government officials would help Jews get passports for a certain amount of money, known as a bribe. This worked for Jews with money, but most were very poor and had to risk sneaking across the Russian border illegally.

These Russian Jews have just arrived in the United States around 1900. They're shown here still on the deck of the crowded ship.

# REACHING AMERICA

In the late 1800s, immigrants to the United States had to cross the Atlantic Ocean in steamships. This journey took up to three weeks. Western Europeans traveled in cabins because they usually had more money. Jewish immigrants had to travel belowdeck because they couldn't afford the more expensive tickets. They slept on iron bunk beds padded with straw. Most of them were too seasick to eat, and there wasn't a lot of drinking water.

When the ships arrived in the United States, the immigrants were taken to Castle Garden, or to Ellis Island after 1891. The U.S. government used these two locations as immigration centers. Immigrants were given medical examinations and questioned to make sure they weren't a danger and could take care of themselves in the United States.

ELLIS ISLAND HOSPITAL

If an immigrant reached the United States, but didn't pass the medical screening, they were often sent to the Ellis Island Immigrant Hospital. After treatment, they were either released or sent back to their home country.

13

# HELP FOR IMMIGRANTS

New immigrants to the United States often had little money or support. Luckily, Jews in the United States and western European countries, such as England, France, and Germany, were willing to help Russian Jews escape persecution.

JEWISH IMMIGRANTS ACCEPT FREE MATZO, OR FLAT BREAD.

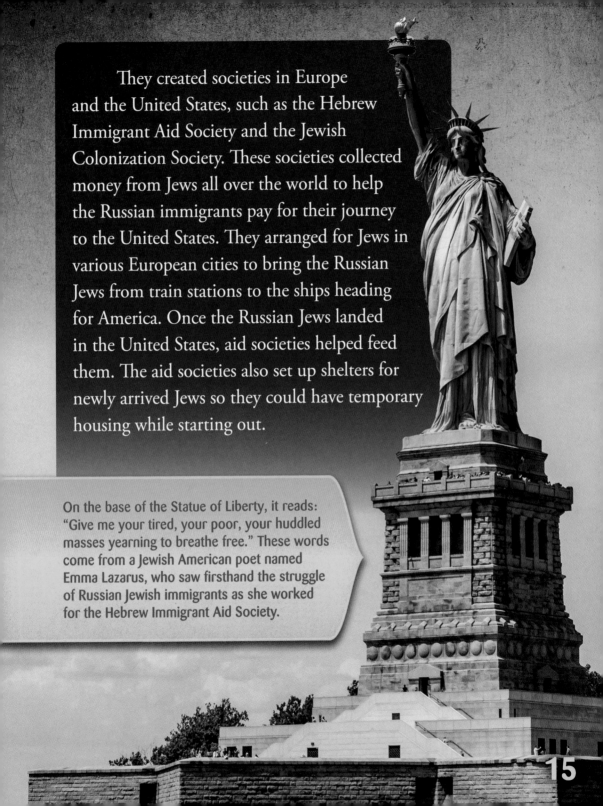

They created societies in Europe and the United States, such as the Hebrew Immigrant Aid Society and the Jewish Colonization Society. These societies collected money from Jews all over the world to help the Russian immigrants pay for their journey to the United States. They arranged for Jews in various European cities to bring the Russian Jews from train stations to the ships heading for America. Once the Russian Jews landed in the United States, aid societies helped feed them. The aid societies also set up shelters for newly arrived Jews so they could have temporary housing while starting out.

On the base of the Statue of Liberty, it reads: "Give me your tired, your poor, your huddled masses yearning to breathe free." These words come from a Jewish American poet named Emma Lazarus, who saw firsthand the struggle of Russian Jewish immigrants as she worked for the Hebrew Immigrant Aid Society.

# FINDING WORK

One of the first things Jewish immigrants looked for in the United States was employment. Many Russian Jewish immigrants worked as **peddlers**. Immigrant aid societies or other friendly Jews in the United States sometimes gave the newly arrived immigrants some money to buy goods to sell. The peddler would then walk around carrying their goods or pushing them on a cart.

Other Jewish immigrants found work in crowded factories. Still others made clothes, a skill which was easy to learn. The garments were made in sweatshops, which were small, dirty rooms full of workers. The sweatshops were often located in the **tenements** where Russian Jews lived. Jews usually worked long hours to make a living, often 12 to 15 hours per day. The crowded rooms were stuffy and hot in warm months and drafty and cold in cold months.

JEWISH MARKET, NEW YORK CITY

This picture shows a Jewish pushcart peddler on a city street. They worked long hours for little pay, just to have enough money to live in a crowded tenement, like the ones pictured on page 16.

# MAKING A NEW HOME

Many Jewish communities already existed in the United States by the time the Russian Jews arrived. In the 1880s, there were already about 250,000 Jews from other parts of the world living in the United States. Most had settled in New York City.

Most of the Jews who came to the United States from Russia in the late 1800s settled in port cities such as Philadelphia, Boston, and New York. Once there, Russian Jews found Jewish communities and places to work.

Large families often packed themselves into one-bedroom apartments in tenements. Many Jewish families lived in tenements on the Lower East Side of Manhattan, which had a large Jewish community.

However, even though they found jobs and a sense of community, there was a period of **adjustment** for Russian Jews. Their housing, especially in tenements, was dirty and run-down. Tenements were also packed with people and often unsafe.

JEWISH TENEMENTS ON EAST BROADWAY IN NEW YORK CITY

# LOOKING TOWARD THE FUTURE

As Russian Jewish immigrants struggled towards success in the United States, they put all they had into the future—their children. Parents worked long hours and saved money so their children could go to school instead of having to work like other immigrant children of the time. The Russian Jews placed a lot of faith in their children. They did everything they could to make sure their children's lives would one day be easier than their own.

"PEOPLE'S THEATRE"
BOWERY & SPRING ST.
SCHULMAN & ROVENGE MGR.
TEL. ORCHARD 0478
MAX ROSENTHAL DIRECTOR
~ NOW PLAYING ~

די צדיק׳ס משפחה

SAMUEL GOLDENBERG
LUDWIG SATZ

IN A SCENE FROM
"THE RABBI'S FAMILY"
WITH AN ALL STAR CAST
TICKETS 4 WEEKS IN ADVANCE

**YIDDISH THEATER POSTER**

Though they looked toward a better future, Russian Jews tried to keep their past alive. They attended Yiddish theater together to provide relief from their hard living conditions. Yiddish theater was a very popular type of drama performed in the Yiddish language. They also practiced their religion together in **synagogues**.

These young Jewish children meet in a small schoolroom to learn about their religion and the history of their people.

# A BETTER LIFE IN AMERICA

Having escaped persecution in Russia, Russian Jews accepted all the challenges they faced in the United States. They joined the Jewish communities that already existed, making them stronger. The Jews in the United States worked hard to make a better life for themselves and their children, and it paid off. Many became successful in their new homes.

Famous **descendants** of Russian Jews include singer-songwriter Bob Dylan and writer Saul Bellow. Other descendants became great actors, such as Dustin Hoffman, James Franco, and Natalie Portman. Some, such as Betty Friedan, were political **activists**. Freed from persecution, Russian Jews could choose how to live, worship, and work. They embraced their new freedom and the hope for a better life in America.

ELDRIDGE STREET SYNAGOGUE, NEW YORK CITY

# GLOSSARY

**activist:** One who acts strongly in support of or against an issue.

**adjustment:** The act or process of changing to fit new conditions.

**anti-Semitism:** Hatred of Jewish people.

**descendant:** A relative of someone from an earlier time.

**discriminate:** To treat people unequally based on class, race, or religion.

**immigrant:** One who comes to a country to settle there.

**passport:** Official papers issued by the government of a country that identify someone as a citizen of that country and are necessary to leave that country and enter another country.

**peddler:** A person who travels around and sells things.

**persecuted:** Treated in a harmful way for being different.

**restrict:** To limit or control.

**synagogue:** A Jewish place of worship.

**temporary:** Lasting for a short amount of time.

**tenement:** A large, poorly kept, and unsafe building that has many apartments or rooms for rent and is usually in a poor part of a city.

**violent:** Having to do with the use of force to harm someone.

# INDEX

# PRIMARY SOURCE LIST

(cover)
A detail from *Food will win the war*. Created by Charles Edward Chambers. Color lithograph poster. Published in 1917. Now kept at the Library of Congress Prints and Photographs Division, Washington, D.C.

p. 5
*Entering the New World*. Created by Charles Joseph Staniland. Illustration. Published originally in the British newspaper *The Graphic* in 1892 and then later that year in the French newspaper *Le Soleil du Dimanche* as *Arrivée d'Émigrants Juifs à New-York*.

pp. 18–19
*Jewish family working on garters in kitchen for tenement home*. Created by Lewis Wickes Hines. Photograph. 1912.

p. 20
*"The Rabbi's Family" at the People's Theater*. Created by Abram Kanof. Poster. 1921.

# WEBSITES